THE
MAGNIFICENT
BOOK OF
MONKEYS
AND APES

THE
MAGNIFICENT
BOOK OF
MONKEYS
AND APES

ILLUSTRATED BY
Simon Treadwell

WRITTEN BY
Barbara Taylor

weldon**owen**

Written by Barbara Taylor
Illustrated by Simon Treadwell

weldon**owen**

Copyright © Weldon Owen Children's Books, 2023

Published by Weldon Owen Children's Books
An imprint of Weldon Owen International, L.P.
A subsidiary of Insight International, L.P.
PO Box 3088
San Rafael, CA 94912
www.insighteditions.com

Designer: Tory Gordon-Harris
Editor: George Maudsley
Senior Production Manager: Greg Steffen

Art Director: Stuart Smith
Publisher: Sue Grabham

CEO: Raoul Goff

ISBN: 978-1-68188-898-9
Manufactured, printed, and assembled in China.
First printing, July 2023. TPO0723
27 26 25 24 23 5 4 3 2 1

Introduction

A huge variety of monkeys and apes climb, swing, and leap through the forests, grasslands, and mountains of our world. Monkeys and apes can look similar, but they are different in important ways. Almost all monkeys have tails, but apes do not. Monkeys are usually smaller and run across branches, while apes are larger and stronger, with long arms and flexible shoulders to swing through the trees.

There are more than 300 kinds of monkey roaming Africa, Asia, and Central and South America. Only one monkey—the Barbary macaque—calls Europe its home. There are far fewer ape species. African apes include chimpanzees, bonobos, and gorillas, while gibbons and orangutans are the Asian apes. No monkeys or apes live in North America or Australasia.

The Magnificent Book of Monkeys and Apes introduces you to some of the most incredible examples of these playful and intelligent animals. Marvel at the red howler—the world's loudest land animal—and see the white-handed gibbon as it hurtles through the trees. Meet the Japanese macaque, which washes its food and has snowball fights, and the chimpanzee, smart enough to make its own weapons. Learn why some apes sing duets, discover which monkey swims underwater and find out how gibbons walk upright along branches at dizzying heights.

Leap into the magnificent realm of monkeys and apes as you explore some of the most fascinating species from across the world.

Fact file

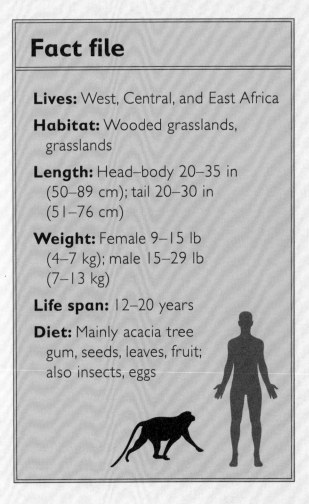

Lives: West, Central, and East Africa

Habitat: Wooded grasslands, grasslands

Length: Head–body 20–35 in (50–89 cm); tail 20–30 in (51–76 cm)

Weight: Female 9–15 lb (4–7 kg); male 15–29 lb (7–13 kg)

Life span: 12–20 years

Diet: Mainly acacia tree gum, seeds, leaves, fruit; also insects, eggs

Contents

Emperor tamarin

Saguinus imperator

- This little South American monkey is only the size of a gray squirrel. It was named 'emperor' after the German ruler Wilhelm II because he had a large mustache.

- During the day, the tamarin moves through the rainforest. It jumps from tree to tree using its long claws to grip the branches. At night, it sleeps huddled with other tamarins inside tree hollows.

- The tamarin's long tail can be up to twice as long as its body. The tail helps it balance as it moves quickly through the treetops.

- This monkey lives in family groups of between two and 20 individuals led by the eldest female. All the monkeys help to care for the young.

- The emperor tamarin lives in the same habitat as the saddleback tamarin. These two species help each other survive by sharing food and watching out for predators.

Fact file

Lives: Northwest South America

Habitat: Rainforests, flooded forests, evergreen forest

Length: Head–body 9–10 in (23–25 cm); tail 14–16 in (35–41 cm)

Weight: 1 lb (450 g)

Life span: 10–20 years

Diet: Fruits, flowers, nectar, tree sap, insects, spiders, eggs, small animals

Sumatran orangutan

Pongo abelii

 Sumatran orangutans are the largest animals that live in trees. They live high up, safe from predators, and rarely come down to the ground.

 Orangutans prefer to live alone, except for a mother and her baby. But some do gather in small groups to feed on fruits such as mangoes and figs.

 An orangutan can usually be spotted slowly swinging its way through the treetops. It uses its hook-shaped fingers and toes to grip the branches.

 Sumatran orangutans sometimes use tools. They poke sticks into termite mounds or bees' nests to lift out insects to eat. They also make gloves out of leaves to protect their hands from prickly fruits or thorny bushes.

An orangutan's long arms span over 6½ feet (2 metres) from one fingertip to the other. That is more than the height of all but the tallest humans! Its arms are so long that they reach the orangutan's ankles when it stands upright.

Fact file

Lives: Sumatra (Indonesia)

Habitat: Rainforests

Height: 4–5 ft (1.2–1.5 m)

Weight: Female 106–121 lb (48–55 kg); male 205–220 lb (93–100 kg)

Life span: 30–40 years

Diet: Fruit, leaves, tree bark, insects, eggs

Japanese macaque

Macaca fuscata

- The Japanese macaque is also known as the snow monkey. This is because some of them live in places where there is snow and ice in winter.

- In the snowy mountains, groups of Japanese macaques keep warm by bathing in hot springs. These are heated by underground volcanic rocks.

- These macaques have large pouches in their cheeks. They store fruit, leaves, and seeds in these pouches, carrying the food to a safe place to eat later.

- Japanese macaques are the only animals apart from humans and raccoons that wash their food before eating it. They sometimes wash food in salt water—scientists think they do this because they enjoy the salty flavor.

 On icy winter nights, macaques sometimes huddle together in the trees to avoid being buried in large drifts of snow on the ground.

 Young Japanese macaques like to play. Sometimes they roll snow into snowballs and the whole troop has a snowball fight.

Fact file

Lives: Japan (Honshu, Kyushu, Skikoku)

Habitat: Warm and cool forests, mountains

Length: Head–body 20–22 in (52–57 cm); tail 2½–4¾ in (7–12 cm)

Weight: Female 12–18 lb (5.5–8 kg); male 22–31 lb (10–14 kg)

Life span: 22–30 years

Diet: Fruit, leaves, seeds, insects, eggs, crabs

Siamang gibbon

Symphalangus syndactylus

The siamang gibbon is a champion acrobat. It uses its extra-long arms to swing effortlessly through the trees.

These gibbons live in small family groups. Every morning, each group sings loudly to warn other siamangs to keep out of their living area.

Siamang parents usually stay together for life, and make a good team. The mother provides the baby with milk, and the father takes over the daily care of the youngster when it is about a year old.

The siamang can grow to almost twice the size of other types of gibbon.

Both male and female siamangs have a throat pouch. This puffs up like a balloon, stretching to the size of a grapefruit. It makes their singing louder so it can be heard up to 2 miles (3 kilometres) away.

Siamangs sometimes walk along branches, stretching their arms over their heads for balance—a bit like a tightrope walker. They do the same when walking on two legs on the ground.

Fact file

Lives: Malaysia, Indonesia, Thailand

Habitat: Tropical rainforests

Height: 29–35 in (74–89 cm)

Weight: Female 20–25 lb (9–11.5 kg); male 23–28 lb (10.5–12.5 kg)

Life span: 25–30 years

Diet: Fruit, leaves, insects, eggs, small animals

Colombian night monkey

Aotus lemurinus

This monkey is the only one in the world that comes out at night.

The Colombian night monkey's huge eyes help it to see well in the dark. They look like an owl's eyes, so another name for this monkey is the gray-bellied owl monkey.

By coming out at night, this monkey avoids predators such as wild cats and birds of prey. It also does not have to compete with daytime monkeys for their favorite food, fruit.

Fact file

Lives: Northwestern South America

Habitat: Rainforests, mountain forests, scrub forests

Length: Head–body 9–19 in (23–48 cm); tail 14½ in (37 cm)

Weight: Female 1¾ lb (860 g); male 2 lb (900 g)

Life span: 20 years

Diet: Fruit, insects, nectar, leaves, birds, bats

During the day, the Colombian night monkey rests in tree hollows, tangles of vines, or other dark places.

When fruit is scarce, the monkey catches the many insects that fly around in the cool, damp night air.

These monkeys keep the same partner for life. To attract a mate, both males and females make hooting calls, rather like an owl.

Silvery marmoset

Mico argentatus

 Silvery marmosets live in family groups of between four and 12 animals. These groups are made up of one adult female, one or more adult males, and young marmosets of different ages.

 These marmosets spend most or all of their lives in the trees. They rarely come down to the ground.

 Twice a year, the group's only female gives birth to twins. Other group members help raise the babies by carrying them through the treetops and finding food for them.

Fact file

Lives: Northeast Brazil

Habitat: Rainforests

Length: Head–body 7–11 in (18–28 cm); tail 10–13 in (26–33 cm)

Weight: Female 14 oz (400 g); male 12 oz (350 g)

Life span: Up to 16 years

Diet: Tree sap and gum, fruit, flowers, frogs, snails, lizards, spiders, insects

With its sharp, chisel-like teeth and long, curved claws, the marmoset digs holes in tree bark. It licks up the sugary sap, gum, or resin that oozes out.

At night, a group of silvery marmosets finds a safe place to sleep. Inside a tree hole or in tangled vegetation, they are safe from predators.

Gelada

Theropithecus gelada

The gelada is the only monkey that eats mainly grass. As grass does not contain many nutrients, a gelada has to eat for about 10 hours a day to get the nourishment it needs.

This monkey has short, strong fingers and gripping thumbs, which help it pick up grass and seeds. Its nimble fingers select only the freshest blades of grass.

The gelada has a brightly colored red patch on its chest. This becomes even brighter when it is ready to mate.

Gelada families sometimes join together to graze peacefully in mega-herds of hundreds, or even as many as 1,200 members. This can only happen because there is enough grass for them to eat on the rich plains of the Ethiopian highlands.

The padded backside of a gelada allows this monkey to shuffle around on its bottom all day picking grass.

When chewing, a gelada's jaws move from side to side, like a cow's or a zebra's. Eating like this helps it grind up the tough grass stems it depends on for survival.

A gelada has an excellent defence against any rival or predator. It flips its top lip inside out over its nostrils to reveal its bright pink gums and large, pointed teeth. It also raises its forehead to show off its unusual pale eyelids.

Fact file

Lives: Ethiopia

Habitat: Mountain grasslands

Length: Head–body 20–29 in (50–74 cm); tail 12–20 in (30–50 cm)

Weight: Female 31 lb (14 kg); male 44 lb (20 kg)

Life span: 14–20 years

Diet: Mainly grass leaves and seeds; also roots, flowers, insects

De Brazza's monkey

Cercopithecus neglectus

This African monkey is named after an Italian explorer. It is also called the swamp monkey because it lives near forested riverbanks and wetlands.

The undersides of this monkey's strong hands and feet are ridged. This allows it to grip the branches of trees, where the monkey spends much of its time.

Groups of up to 10 De Brazza's monkeys are led by a male. The males are almost twice the size of the females.

De Brazza's babies are born with golden fur. They start to grow a white beard and mustache when they are six weeks old, and are the same color as the adults by the age of six months.

Not all monkeys can see every color. De Brazza's monkeys can see the color red, which helps them to find ripe fruit easily.

If these shy monkeys sense danger, most hide and stay silent until it has passed. They may curl up into a ball and stay still for hours.

Fact file

Lives: Central Africa

Habitat: Swamp forest, tropical forest, mountain forest

Length: Head–body 16–25 in (40–64 cm); tail 20–29 in (51–74 cm)

Weight: Female 9 lb (4 kg); male 17 lb (7.7 kg)

Life span: 20–26 years

Diet: Mainly fruit; also leaves, mushrooms, insects

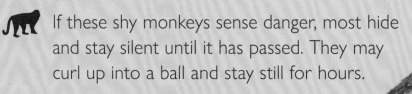

Patas monkey

Erythrocebus patas

The patas monkey is the fastest monkey in the world. Its powerful back legs help it run away from predators at up to 34 mph (55 kph)—that's much faster than record-breaking human sprinters.

Every day, the patas monkey travels long distances on a never-ending search for food and water. Its long legs allow it to range over large areas of grassland without using too much energy.

The males protect their troop of up to 40 monkeys from predators. Their alarm calls warn of nearby danger and lure dangerous animals away. This gives the females and young time to hide.

The male patas monkey's pointed canine teeth are nearly twice the length of the females' canines. Males use theirs for display and fighting rivals.

The patas monkey is sometimes called the military monkey. Its red coat and white mustache make it look a bit like an old-fashioned soldier.

This monkey has an unusual hunting technique for catching flying insects. It stands up and swipes at them with one hand, or even leaps straight up in the air to catch them.

Fact file

Lives: West, Central and East Africa

Habitat: Wooded grasslands, grasslands

Length: Head–body 20–35 in (50–89 cm); tail 20–30 in (51–76 cm)

Weight: Female 9–15 lb (4–7 kg); male 15–29 lb (7–13 kg)

Life span: 12–20 years

Diet: Mainly acacia tree gum, seeds, leaves, fruit; also insects, eggs

Drill

Mandrillus leucophaeus

The powerful, short-tailed male drill is one of the world's largest monkeys. The female is only about half its size.

Drills live in groups of about 20 monkeys. Each group is led by a powerful male. Sometimes groups join together to form a supergroup of up to 100 drills.

In the breeding season, drills rub their chests against trees to spread their scent and mark their territory.

These monkeys spend a lot of time grooming each other's fur. This strengthens the bonds between group members. It also keeps the drills healthy by removing dirt, dead skin, and blood-sucking bugs.

A drill walks with its hands flat on the ground. This is unlike great apes such as chimpanzees or gorillas, which walk on the knuckles of their hands.

The male drill becomes more colorful as he gets older. He develops a red chin and a red, pink, and blue bottom. As well as attracting mates, these bright colors may also help a group to stay together in the dim forest light.

Fact file

Lives: West Africa

Habitat: Rainforests

Length: Head–body 22 in (56 cm);
tail 2–3 in (5–8 cm)

Weight: Female 26–45 lb (12–20 kg);
male 70–110 lb (32–50 kg)

Life span: 20 years

Diet: Mainly fruits; also
seeds, insects, plants,
eggs, small mammals

Proboscis monkey

Nasalis larvatus

Up in the trees, the male proboscis monkey lets out its honking call. This monkey is known for its enormous nose, which hangs over its mouth. Scientists think its nose makes its cry louder, and that it uses this cry to try to attract females.

The proboscis monkey has a large pot belly. This space for its large stomach helps it digest the tough leaves it eats. Sometimes the monkey coughs up its food and then chews it again to break down the leaves.

This monkey is a great swimmer. Its webbed fingers and partly webbed toes help it swim across deep rivers to find food or escape danger.

A baby proboscis monkey is born with a blue face and black fur. It develops its adult colors when it is about three or four months old.

The proboscis monkey has a special skill—it can swim underwater! It dives as deep as 65 feet (20 metres) below the surface.

This monkey's tail is as long as its body. It helps the monkey balance as it leaps through the treetops.

Fact file

Lives: Borneo

Habitat: Mangrove forests, lowland rainforests, swamps

Length: Head–body 21–30 in (53–76 cm); tail 20–29 in (52–74 cm)

Weight: Female 15–26 lb (7–12 kg); male 35–50 lb (16–23 kg)

Life span: 15–20 years

Diet: Mainly leaves, fruit; also seeds, bark, flowers, insects

Western lowland gorilla

Gorilla gorilla gorilla

This baby western lowland gorilla weighed a tiny 4 pounds (2 kilograms) at birth, which is less than most human babies. Mothers have one baby at a time, and carry them around on their backs.

This gorilla is the most common of the four types of gorilla. Yet there are probably less than 100,000 of this species left because of hunting, habitat destruction, and the diseases they catch from people.

Although they are usually gentle giants, male western lowland gorillas sometimes have violent fights over females, or roar and pound their huge chests to scare off attackers.

Fact file

Lives: Central and West Africa

Habitat: Lowland tropical rainforests, swamp forests

Height: Female 4 ft 7 in (1.4 m); male 5 ft 11 in (1.8 m)

Weight: Female 154–308 lb (70–140 kg); male 308–401 lb (140–182 kg)

Life span: 35–40 years

Diet: Leafy plants, fruit, bark, roots, insects

These great apes communicate with each other in all kinds of ways. They use a variety of sounds, as well as touch, face, and body movements.

All gorillas over three years old create nests from branches and leaves. Females and their young build their nests up on strong tree branches, but big, heavy males make theirs on the ground.

31

Pygmy marmoset

Cebuella pygmaea

- The pygmy marmoset is the world's smallest monkey. It is so tiny it can fit into the palm of a human's hand.

- Strong, claw-shaped nails allow the marmoset to grip branches as it scampers about the treetops. Its tail is longer than its body and helps it to balance.

- Sugary tree sap is this marmoset's favorite food. Its sharp bottom teeth chew small holes in tree bark so the sticky sap leaks out. Just a few trees provide a family with all the sap it needs.

Each newborn pygmy marmoset is only as big as a human thumb. For the first two weeks of their lives, the babies ride around on their fathers' backs.

A pygmy marmoset can leap long distances of up to 16 feet (5 metres) in a single bound when threatened. Rainforest predators include pit vipers and small cats such as ocelots and margays.

Fact file

Lives: Northwest South America

Habitat: Tropical rainforests

Length: Head–body 4¾–6¼ in (12–16 cm); tail 6¾–9 in (17–23 cm)

Weight: Female 4¼ oz (120 g); male 3¾ oz (110 g)

Life span: 8–12 years

Diet: Tree sap, fruit, insects

Barbary macaque

Macaca sylvanus

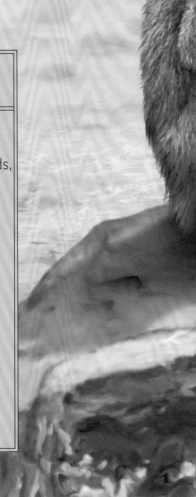

The Barbary macaque is the only monkey found in the wild in Europe, where it lives in Gibraltar on the coast of southern Spain. It can also be found in northwest Africa's Barbary Coast, the area that gives it its name.

Each Barbary macaque has a different call. A mother can find her baby by listening for its unique cry.

This macaque has large, stretchy cheek pouches that extend down the sides of its neck. They are used to carry food, and can hold nearly as much as the monkey's stomach.

Unlike most other monkeys, Barbary macaques only have a tiny stub of a tail. This helps them to walk on the ground on all fours without their tail getting in the way.

Fact file

Lives: Morocco, Algeria, Gibraltar

Habitat: Mountain forests, grasslands, scrub, rocky cliffs

Length: Head–body 18–28 in (45–71 cm); tail ½–1 in (1–2 cm)

Weight: Female 11–20 lb (5–9 kg); male 15–27 lb (7–12 kg)

Life span: 22–30 years

Diet: Leaves, fruit, seeds, berries, insects, lizards, frogs, worms

The Barbary macaque is one of the few monkeys to live in cold and snowy places. Its thick fur helps it keep warm in winter.

Barbary macaques are endangered. They are at risk of dying out in the wild in the next 10–15 years because of habitat loss, climate change, and being caught to be sold as pets.

Hamadryas baboon

Papio hamadryas

These big, sturdy monkeys have strong brows, a long, doglike snout, and large, sharp teeth.

Male hamadryas baboons have thick, silvery manes of fur on their head and back. Females have no mane and short, brownish fur.

The ancient Egyptians believed that hamadryas baboons were sacred to Thoth, the god of learning. They even preserved some of these baboons by mummifying their bodies.

Travelling in large groups helps to protect these baboons from predators.

 Sitting pads allow hamadryas baboons to sit for long periods of time. The pads are also useful at night when they sleep on rocky cliff edges to stay safe from predators.

 Baby hamadryas baboons are born with black fur. They are about the size of a guinea pig and ride around on their mother's back. Males play with their young and protect them.

Fact file

Lives: Northeast Africa, southwest Saudi Arabia, Yemen

Habitat: Mountains, grasslands, rocky deserts, dry brushland

Length: Head–body 20–37 in (50–95 cm); tail 15–24 in (37–60 cm)

Weight: Female 20–24 lb (9–11 kg); male 40–44 lb (18–20 kg)

Life span: 20–30 years

Diet: Seeds, roots, berries, leaves, insects, eggs

Sooty mangabey

Cercocebus atys

The sooty mangabey is named for the sooty, ash-gray color of its fur. It is also known as the white-collared mangabey because of the white collar of fur under its chin.

With its powerful jaws and teeth, these monkeys bite into hard fruits and seeds, or tear bark from trees. The females have smaller front teeth so eat softer seeds, fruits, and insects.

A sooty mangabey is good at spotting predators such as leopards or chimpanzees. It will give a loud alarm call if it sees one approaching and uses different alarm calls for different predators.

These monkeys lower and raise their bright white eyelids to communicate with each other. Batting eyelids quickly is a warning to other sooty mangabeys.

Sooty mangabeys sometimes live in mixed groups with other monkeys, such as red colobus and Diana monkeys. The sooty mangabeys' warning alarm calls help keep them all safe from predators.

Fact file

Lives: West Africa

Habitat: Tropical forests, flooded forests, mangrove forests

Length: Head–body 16–26 in (41–66 cm); tail 16–24 in (41–61 cm)

Weight: Female 10–15 lb (4.5–7 kg); male 15–26 lb (7–12 kg)

Life span: 18–26 years

Diet: Fruits, nuts, seeds, insects

Vervet monkey

Chlorocebus pygerythrus

 Vervet monkeys rely on acacia trees both for food and places to sleep. The acacia's spiny branches provide protection from predators, such as leopards, pythons, baboons, and African crowned eagles.

 Tree gum is an important part of a vervet's diet. It scrapes the sticky gum off the bark of the acacia tree with its mouth.

 This small monkey has long arms and legs. These provide the speed and agility to scamper away from large predators on the ground. In the trees, its long tail helps it to balance.

 Young vervet monkeys often play with each other. By doing this, they test their strength and learn how to live in a group. This training helps them to defend themselves when they grow up.

Fact file

Lives: East and South Africa

Habitat: Grasslands, woodlands, urban

Length: Head–body 18–20 in (45–50 cm); tail 20–30 in (50–75 cm)

Weight: Female 7½–11¾ lb (3.4–5.3 kg); male 8½–17¾ lb (3.9–8 kg)

Life span: 12–18 years

Diet: Mainly acacia leaves, flowers, gum, pods, bark; also insects, small animals

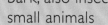

Vervet monkeys sometimes go into villages and towns to feed on human leftovers. They may even break into houses to help themselves to food.

Members of a vervet troop regularly groom each other's fur for bugs and dirt. This keeps them healthy and helps the troop learn to work together.

Bonobo

Pan paniscus

The bonobo is closely related to chimpanzees and humans. They are all part of the great ape family, which also includes gorillas and orangutans.

These apes live in peaceful troops of 30–100 members. They split up to feed and travel in smaller groups of up to 15.

The bonobo swings effortlessly from tree to tree searching for fruit and leaves to eat. It also spends time gathering food on the ground, often sharing what it finds with others in the troop.

Males may be larger and stronger, but it is the females that hold the most important positions in bonobo troops. They gain power by teaming up with other females.

Every evening, bonobos use leaves and twigs to build nests in the trees. Adults sometimes share a nest, something that is unique among the great apes.

At night, bonobos are good at looking out for each other. They keep a watch for predators, such as snakes or leopards, which might creep up on them.

Wars, illegal hunting, and people cutting down the forests where they live are all endangering bobonos. Their numbers are falling, and scientists think there are only 10,000–20,000 left in the wild.

Fact file

Lives: Democratic Republic of Congo

Habitat: Lowland rainforests

Height: 3 ft 9 in (1.15 m)

Weight: Female 68 lb (31 kg); male 86 lb (39 kg)

Life span: 20–40 years

Diet: Fruit, seeds, leaves, flowers, small animals

Golden snub-nosed monkey

Rhinopithecus roxellana

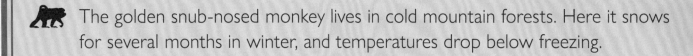 The golden snub-nosed monkey lives in cold mountain forests. Here it snows for several months in winter, and temperatures drop below freezing.

In autumn, the golden snub-nosed monkey grows a thick coat that helps it to keep warm in the cold. In spring, this is replaced by shorter fur, so the monkey stays cool in the warmer summer months.

The golden snub-nosed monkey's furry tail is thickly padded. It acts like a soft cushion when it sits on it.

In summer, golden snub-nosed monkeys live in large groups of 200–600 members, which helps them to fight off predators, such as wolves, birds of prey, and leopards. In winter they split into smaller troops of less than 40.

To communicate, this monkey makes a variety of calls. It can even produce sounds without moving its mouth, like a human ventriloquist.

Fact file

Lives: China

Habitat: Mountain forests

Length: Head–body 20–30 in (51–76 cm); tail 20–28 in (51–71 cm)

Weight: Female 14¼–22 lb (6.5–10 kg); male 33–86 lb (15–39 kg)

Life span: 20–25 years

Diet: Pine needles, bamboo shoots, leaves, flowers, fruits, seeds, lichens

This monkey's snub nose may be that shape because it is less likely to get frostbitten in freezing weather.

45

Black-handed spider monkey

Ateles geoffroyi

This monkey's long, thin limbs look like the legs of a spider, which is how it gets its name. Its arms are even longer than its legs.

The black-handed spider monkey's long tail works like an extra hand, curling around branches for support. This agile monkey can hang by its tail alone, and even use it to pick fruit and throw things.

With its long, hooklike fingers and flexible shoulders, the black-handed spider monkey swings easily arm over arm from branch to branch. This way of moving quickly through the treetops is called brachiation.

The monkey's tail is very strong. There is also a fleshy pad under the tail that is unique to each monkey, a bit like a human fingerprint.

Adult black-handed spider monkeys look after their young for three years. The adults even use their bodies to make bridges in the trees for youngsters to walk across until they are ready to leap across themselves.

If it is threatened, the black-handed spider monkey barks loudly, throws or shakes branches, and jumps up and down to scare predators away.

These monkeys have good memories. They learn to identify different types of fruit tree, and can remember where to find them in the forest.

Fact file

Lives: Central America

Habitat: Rainforests, mountain forests, mangrove forests

Length: Head–body 12–24 in (30–60 cm); tail 25–34 in (64–86 cm)

Weight: Female 13–18 lb (6–8 kg); male 16–20 lb (7.5–9 kg)

Life span: 24–27 years

Diet: Mainly fruit; also leaves, flowers, nuts, seeds, insects, spiders, eggs

Guereza colobus

Colobus guereza

The guereza colobus lives in troops of up to 15 monkeys, usually led by a male. The females have the most important roles in the troop, helping each other to look after the babies and young monkeys.

This monkey has a black body with a long white mantle of fur that stretches from its shoulder to its hip. Scientists think that the mantle and the long, fluffy tail act together like a parachute, spreading out as the colobus jumps between trees. Its tail helps it change direction as it leaps.

The guereza spends more than half its day resting, and the remaining daylight hours grooming other guerezas and searching for food.

Fact file

Lives: Central Africa

Habitat: Rainforests, swamp forests, mountain forests, grassy woodlands

Length: Head–body 20–27 in (50–70 cm); tail 26–26¾ in (66–68 cm)

Weight: Female 17–20 lb (7.5–9 kg); male 20–30 lb (9–13.5 kg)

Life span: 20–22 years

Diet: Mainly leaves, fruit; also bark, seeds

Newborn guerezas are white with a pink face. The babies start to change color when they are about one month old, and become black and white by the time they are three months old.

The guereza treats bendy branches like trampolines. It jumps up and down on them before launching itself across gaps in the trees for up to 50 feet (15 metres), more than the length of a bus!

A colobus's four long fingers help it grip branches and move easily through the treetops. Unlike most other monkeys, it has only tiny thumbs or no thumbs at all so they do not get in this monkey's way.

Allen's swamp monkey

Allenopithecus nigroviridis

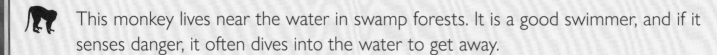 This monkey lives near the water in swamp forests. It is a good swimmer, and if it senses danger, it often dives into the water to get away.

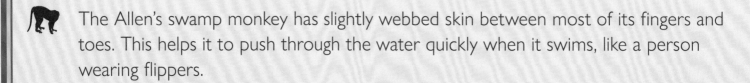 The Allen's swamp monkey has slightly webbed skin between most of its fingers and toes. This helps it to push through the water quickly when it swims, like a person wearing flippers.

By day, groups of up to 40 Allen's swamp monkeys hunt for food on the ground. At night, they gather in trees near riverbanks to sleep. They use loud, chirping alarm calls to warn each other of danger from predators.

Allen's swamp monkeys like a wide range of foods, although they eat more small animals—such as caterpillars, snails, and fish—than other monkeys.

Fact file

Lives: Central Africa

Habitat: Swamp forests

Length: Head–body 18–24 in (46–61 cm); tail 20 in (50 cm)

Weight: Female 8 lb (3.7 kg); male 13 lb (6 kg)

Life span: 18–20 years

Diet: Fruit, nuts, leaves, flowers, seeds, insects, fish, shrimps, snails

This monkey has an unusual hunting technique. It sometimes puts leaves or grass on the surface of the water and then snatches up the fish that hide in the shade of the floating plants.

 A male Allen's swamp monkey has scent glands on its chest. It rubs scent from these glands onto tree trunks and branches. Scientists think this is to mark its territory.

Red howler

Alouatta seniculus

The loudest of all land animals, male red howlers wake up the forest with an early-morning chorus of deafening howls. They also howl at night before they go to sleep. Their calls can be heard up to 3 miles (5 kilometres) away.

Howling helps groups of these monkeys to space themselves out in the forest. It tells them where other red howler groups are so they can keep away from them to avoid fights over food.

The red howler spends most of its life in the treetops, where there are plenty of fresh young leaves. Its large jaws allow it to chew the tough leaves thoroughly, while bacteria in its gut help it to digest its food.

Red howlers have a prehensile, or gripping, tail. They use the tail like an extra hand to grasp branches, leaving their hands free to collect food.

Fact file

Lives: Northwest South America

Habitat: Rainforests, tropical forests, swamp forests

Length: Head–body 18–28 in (46–71 cm); tail 20–30 in (50–75 cm)

Weight: Female 10–14 lb (4.5–6.3 kg); male 13–17 lb (6–7.6 kg)

Life span: 15–20 years

Diet: Mainly leaves; also fruits, flowers, seeds

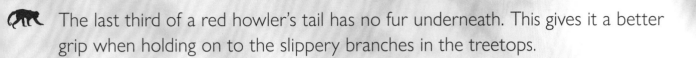 The last third of a red howler's tail has no fur underneath. This gives it a better grip when holding on to the slippery branches in the treetops.

A troop of red howlers is led by a male and contains 10–13 monkeys. Members of the troop groom each other to strengthen the close bonds between them.

Chimpanzee

Pan troglodytes

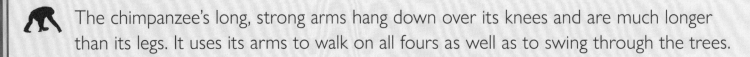

The chimpanzee's long, strong arms hang down over its knees and are much longer than its legs. It uses its arms to walk on all fours as well as to swing through the trees.

These apes use tools when they are hunting or finding food. They smash open nuts with stones and soak up water to drink using leaves. They also poke twigs or grass stems into termite mounds to get insects to eat.

Every night, chimps bend and weave branches into new sleeping nests.

A small group of chimpanzees sometimes works together to hunt animals. Before setting off, some of them will snap off branches and use their teeth to sharpen them into pointed spears.

Chimpanzees use a wide variety of different calls to keep in touch with members of their community. They laugh when they play, hoot when they discover food, and scream when they are excited.

Fact file

Lives: West and Central Africa

Habitat: Rainforests, mountain forests, grasslands

Length: 4 ft 3 in–5 ft 3 in (1.3–1.6 m)

Weight: Female 71–104 lb (32–47 kg); male 88–132 lb (40–60 kg)

Life span: 45–50 years

Diet: Fruits, leaves, seeds, nuts, insects, mammals

Sadly, chimpanzees are highly endangered by people killing them for meat, destroying their habitat, and capturing them to sell as pets. They could die out in the wild within the next few decades.

Masked titi

Callicebus personatus

The masked titi only lives in a particular area of coastal rainforest in Brazil. People have cut down most of its forest home, so it is under threat of extinction.

This small monkey is similar in size to a rabbit, and the male and female titi look alike. The male is only slightly larger than the female.

Masked titis live in small family groups, which are made up of a pair of titis and their young. A pair of masked titis usually stay together for life.

The male masked titi takes over the care of the young when they are about one week old. Fathers carry the babies around until the young can fend for themselves.

At night, groups of masked titis sleep huddled in tall trees, with their tails twined together. This helps to strengthen the bonds between the members of a group.

Masked titis sometimes eat soil, but scientists are not sure why they do this. It may be because the soil contains useful minerals, or it may help them digest food or eat toxic plants without getting poisoned.

Fact file

Lives: Southeastern Brazil

Habitat: Coastal rainforests

Length: Head–body 12–16 in (30–41 cm); tail 16–22 in (41–56 cm)

Weight: Female 2–3½ lb (1–1.6 kg); male 2½–4 lb (1.1–1.7 kg)

Life span: 20–25 years

Diet: Mainly fruit; also seeds, leaves, birds' eggs, insects, small animals

White-handed gibbon

Hylobates lar

The agile white-handed gibbon is the great gymnast of the ape world. It can swing arm-over-arm through the treetops at more than 35 mph (55 kph). That is even faster than a champion Olympic sprinter!

This gibbon gets its name from the white fur on the tops of its hands and feet.

When sleeping, the white-handed gibbon sits upright in the tree forks of tall trees. It keeps as quiet as possible to avoid attracting predators, such as clouded leopards and pythons.

This gibbon eats a lot of fruit, especially figs. The droppings it leaves behind help spread the seeds of these forest plants.

The white-handed gibbon is a threatened species because people hunt it for food or to be sold as a pet. Its forest habitat is also being destroyed, so it has fewer places to live.

This gibbon can jump huge distances between branches. It can even leap up to catch birds and insects in midair.

Fact file

Lives: Southern and Southeast Asia

Habitat: Tropical and subtropical forests

Length: 17–23 in (43–58 cm)

Weight: Female 10–15 lb (4.5–7 kg); male 11–17 lb (5–7.5 kg)

Life span: 20–30 years

Diet: Fruit, leaves, flowers, insects, eggs, birds

Common squirrel monkey

Saimiri sciureus

 These small monkeys are named for the fast, agile way they climb and leap through the trees, just like a squirrel. They spend nearly all of their time in the trees and rarely go down to the ground.

 Squirrel monkeys rub their hands and feet with their own urine. This helps them control their body temperature and allows them to leave scent trails for the rest of their large troop to follow.

 Flexible fingers and sharp fingernails are used to peel the fruit this monkey eats. They are also useful when catching insect prey.

Fact file

Lives: Northeastern South America

Habitat: Rainforests

Length: Head–body 12½ in (32 cm); tail 15¾ in (40 cm)

Weight: Female 1½–2¾ lb (650–1250 g); male 1¼–2½ lb (550–1150 g)

Life span: 15–20 years

Diet: Mainly fruit; also leaves, seeds, insects, bats, birds

Sometimes squirrel monkeys work with their close relatives the capuchin monkeys to find food and watch out for predators.

Common squirrel monkeys have a pointed white arch above their eyes. Their white face markings look a bit like a skull, so they are sometimes also called skull monkeys or death's head monkeys.

White-faced capuchin

Cebus capucinus

 The white-faced capuchin is good at using tools. It overturns rocks with branches to find insects, cracks open and mashes hard fruit with stones, and defends itself against snakes with sticks.

 This noisy monkey makes loud calls to warn others in its troop of danger, such as predators or rival troops. Different calls are used to keep in touch and to tell the troop to move in a different direction.

 When the white-faced capuchin sticks out its tongue, it is not being rude. It is actually allowing moisture to escape, which helps the monkey to stay cool in the hot, steamy forest.

 Like all capuchins, this one rubs parts of certain plants into its fur. This could be to repel insects or fungi, or it may be a medicine to treat wounds or bites.

 When they are thirsty, white-faced capuchins drink water trapped inside the cup-shaped leaves of bromeliad plants. These plants are located high in the trees of the monkey's rainforest home.

Fact file

Lives: Central America, northwest South America

Habitat: Rainforests, mangrove forests, mountain forests

Length: Head–body 13–18 in (33–46 cm); tail 22 in (55 cm)

Weight: Female 4½–6½ lb (2–3 kg); male 6½–9 lb (3–4 kg)

Life span: 20–30 years

Diet: Mainly fruit, nuts; also leaves, seeds, insects, birds, lizards

Bald uakari

Cacajao calvus

The bald uakari's (*wah-kar-ee*) bright, pink-red face is a sign of good health. Its face may become brighter when it is excited or angry. Females prefer males with very red faces.

This monkey may travel up to 3 miles (5 kilometres) in just one day. It usually walks and runs on all fours, but sometimes walks and jumps on two legs on the forest floor.

The powerful jaws and long, sharp fangs of a bald uakari help it to bite through thick fruit skins and hard nuts.

Strong back legs allow the bald uakari to jump distances of up to 65 feet (20 metres) from tree to tree.

The bald uakari has the shortest tail of all the South American monkeys. When it is excited or threatened, it may wag its tail like a dog.

The deep red of the bald uakari's face is caused by a lot of blood flowing just beneath the skin. A pale face shows that the monkey probably has a disease called malaria. This is spread by mosquitoes, which are common in the wet, swampy forests where these monkeys live.

Fact file

Lives: Eastern Peru and western Brazil

Habitat: Swampy tropical rainforests

Length: Head–body 15–22 in (38–56 cm); tail 6 in (15 cm)

Weight: Female 5½ lb (2.5 kg); male 6½ lb (3 kg)

Life span: 15–20 years

Diet: Leaves, fruit, seeds, roots, insects

Hanuman langur

Semnopithecus entellus

The Hanuman langur is one of the tamest monkeys in the world. It is not afraid of people and often lives in villages, towns, and cities.

This gray langur is named after the Hindu monkey god, Lord Hanuman. The monkey is treated as a sacred animal in the Hindu religion.

Hanuman langurs are excellent climbers, and their long tails help them to balance on branches, cliffs, and rooftops.

Leaves make up about half of a Hanuman langur's diet. It is able to digest tough leaves easily and can eat seeds that might poison other animals.

The Hanuman langur is very agile. It can leap 30–50 feet (10–15 metres) in one bound and can even jump 16 feet (5 metres) into the air.

Fact file

Lives: India, Bangladesh, Sri Lanka, Nepal, Bhutan, Pakistan

Habitat: Rainforests, deserts, grasslands, scrub, mountains, urban

Length: Head–body 18–31 in (45–79 cm); tail 27–40 in (70–100 cm)

Weight: Female 26 lb (12 kg); male 37 lb (17 kg)

Life span: 18–30 years

Diet: Fruits, flowers, leaves, insects

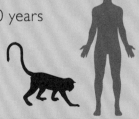

Hanuman langurs communicate with a variety of barks, coughs, grunts, and whoops. The males' loud whoops can be heard over 1 mile (2 kilometres) away.

The Hanuman langur's habitat is decreasing as people grow crops, graze animals, build towns, and mine the land where these monkeys live.

Common woolly monkey

Lagothrix lagotricha

 The common woolly monkey spends most of its time high in the trees. Its long prehensile, or gripping, tail tightly curls and uncurls around branches to stop the monkey falling as it moves through the trees.

 These large, muscular monkeys are named for their soft, thick fur, which looks a bit like sheep's wool.

 The woolly monkey lives in groups of between 10 and 70 males and females. They are a peaceful species and often share space with other woolly monkey groups living nearby.

Fact file

Lives: Northern South America

Habitat: Rainforests, flooded tropical forests

Length: Head–body 16–24 in (40–60 cm); tail 24–28 in (60–71 cm)

Weight: Female 13 lb (6 kg); male 20 lb (9 kg)

Life span: 25–30 years

Diet: Mainly fruit; also leaves, nuts, insects, small animals

Several national parks and reserves in South America are working hard to protect common woolly monkeys. These monkeys are also kept safe by laws against catching and selling endangered species.

The thick coat of the common woolly monkey helps to protect it from rain and strong sunshine, as well as insect bites and stings.

White-faced saki

Pithecia pithecia

Male and female white-faced sakis sing duets to strengthen their bond and defend their territory from rival groups. Their songs include trills, chuckles, whistles, and growls.

The sakis have powerful bodies and strong leg muscles. Huge leaps of 30 feet (10 metres) carry them from tree to tree and have earned them the nickname flying monkey.

Male and female sakis look very different. The male has a white face and long, black fur, while the female has gray and brown fur. Their thick fur helps them to stay dry during heavy forest rains.

The white-faced saki's thick, bushy tail is as long as its body.

White-faced sakis drink by dipping their hands into pools of water that collect in tree hollows. They then lick the water off their hands.

Sakis' long, thin fingers and toes have thick pads on their tips. These help them to grip branches easily as they leap through the treetops.

Fact file

Lives: Northeastern South America

Habitat: Rainforests

Length: Head–body 12–16 in (30–40 cm); tail 12–16½ in (30–42 cm)

Weight: Female 3–4¼ lb (1.4–2 kg); male 4–5¼ lb (2–2.5 kg)

Life span: 15 years

Diet: Mainly fruits and seeds; also leaves, flowers, insects

Red-shanked douc langur

Pygathrix nemaeuss

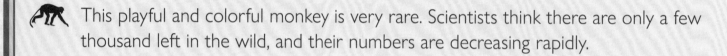

This playful and colorful monkey is very rare. Scientists think there are only a few thousand left in the wild, and their numbers are decreasing rapidly.

"Douc" is a very old Vietnamese word, which is thought to mean monkey. "Shanked" refers to the monkey's legs, which are red from the knee down.

The douc langur's big belly contains a stomach with many chambers, like a cow's. Bacteria in the langur's stomach break down the tough leaves that it eats. This process creates gases that make the langur burp.

Adult monkeys of any kind do not usually share food, although mothers may share food with their young. Douc langurs are unusual because they eat together peacefully and will share food with other members of their troop.

Fact file

Lives: Laos, Vietnam, Cambodia

Habitat: Rainforests, monsoon forests

Length: Head–body 22–24 in (56–61 cm); tail 24–29 in (61–74 cm)

Weight: Female 18–20 lb (8–9 kg); male 24–28 lb (11–12.5 kg)

Life span: 25 years

Diet: Mainly leaves; also seeds, flowers, fruit

When males and females are ready to mate, they push their jaws forward, wiggle their eyebrows up and down, and shake their heads.

 Both male and female red-shanked douc langurs eventually leave the groups they were born into.

 Red-shanked douc langurs prefer to eat fruit that is not quite ripe. This is because ripe fruit upsets their stomachs.

Bonnet macaque

Macaca radiata

These macaques are named after the cap of parted hair on their heads. Their hair makes them look like they are wearing an old-fashioned hat called a bonnet.

Sometimes bonnet macaques eat the soil from termite nests. This is thought to help them cure an upset stomach.

Male and female bonnet macaques live together in troops of up to 30. The males born into the group usually leave when they become adults, but the females stay with the group.

These fast and quick-witted macaques often steal food from houses, food stalls, and piles of rubbish. They also take food people have left as offerings at temples.

Fact file

Lives: Southern India

Habitat: Forests, grasslands, urban

Length: Head–body 14–23 in (35–59 cm); tail 3½–6¼ in (9–16 cm)

Weight: Female 8½ lb (4 kg); male 15 lb (7 kg)

Life span: 20–25 years

Diet: Fruit, nuts, seeds, leaves, berries, insects, small animals, eggs

All the monkeys in a bonnet macaque troop groom each other's fur, even the most important males. This is rare, because higher-ranking monkeys do not usually groom lower-ranking ones.

The monkeys are unusual because the adult males play with their young. The young leap, wrestle with, and pretend to attack the adults. This behavior teaches them how to survive when they grow up.

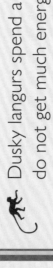

Dusky langur

Trachypithecus obscurus

- This langur is sometimes called the spectacled leaf monkey, because its white eye rings look like glasses, or spectacles, and its main food is leaves.

- Strongs hands and feet give the gray-furred dusky langur a tight grasp on branches, while its long tail helps it balance as it leaps through the trees.

- The dusky langur's eyes face forward, which helps it judge depths and distances up in the trees.

- Mother dusky langurs chew leaves before feeding them to their young. This breaks down the food, making it easier for the young langurs to digest.

- Dusky langurs spend a lot of time resting, as they do not get much energy from their leafy diet. This may be why they are very peaceful and calm compared to other monkeys.

Sometimes dusky langurs chase each other and play games. They wrestle, run about, and pull each other's tails.

Newborn dusky langurs have bright yellow or orange fur. They develop their dusky adult colors by the time they are six months old.

Fact file

Lives: Malaysia, Myanmar, Thailand

Habitat: Forests, national parks, urban areas

Length: Head–body 17–24 in (43–61 cm); tail 20–33 in (50–84 cm)

Weight: Female 14 lb (6.5 kg); male 16 lb (7.3 kg)

Life span: 25 years

Diet: Mainly leaves; also shoots, flowers, fruit

Golden lion tamarin

Leontopithecus rosalia

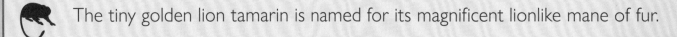 The tiny golden lion tamarin is named for its magnificent lionlike mane of fur.

The long, slender fingers of the golden lion tamarin have clawlike nails. The monkey uses them to search out prey in holes or cracks in bark and plants.

These tamarins live in groups of between two and eight family members. Everyone in the group helps to carry and look after the babies, but it is the adult male that is the main caregiver.

Each group of golden lion tamarins lives in its own special area of forest. The tamarins use scent and calls to mark this territory, which they defend fiercely from other golden lion tamarins.

Golden lion tamarins are a rare and endangered species. They are threatened by the destruction of their forest home for wood or the building of farms or towns.

Fact file

Lives: Southeastern Brazil

Habitat: Coastal rainforests

Length: Head–body 7½–8¾ in (19–22 cm); tail 10¼–13 in (26–33 cm)

Weight: 17–24 oz (480–680 g)

Life span: 8–15 years

Diet: Fruit, flowers, plant sap, birds' eggs, insects, lizards, frogs

Monkeys and Apes Around the World